# Protecting Young Students and Children from Cyber Threats: A Comprehensive Guide to Online Safety

Dr. Abdulrahman Abdullah Alghamdi

In today's digital world, children and students are increasingly vulnerable to a wide range of cyber threats, from phishing scams and malware attacks to cyberbullying and identity theft. This book is designed to raise awareness about the dangers of cybercrime and to empower teachers, parents, and students with the skills and knowledge they need to stay safe online.

Through comprehensive coverage of all the key aspects of online safety, including the latest technology and trends, this book offers a balanced perspective on the benefits and risks of technology. It provides practical tips and advice for preventing cyber attacks and protecting sensitive information, as well as promoting critical thinking and digital literacy skills to help children and students navigate the digital world in a safe and responsible manner.

With a focus on empowering young students and children with the skills and knowledge they need to stay safe online, now and in the future, this book offers a comprehensive guide to online safety. From the role of teachers and parents in protecting students, to the importance of cyber safety education in schools and institutions, this book covers all the essential information you need to stay safe and secure online.

Whether you are a teacher, parent, or student, this book is an essential resource for anyone looking to protect themselves and their loved ones from cyber threats. So why wait? Start reading today and take the first step towards a safer, more secure digital world.

Dr. Abdulrahman Alghamdi
College of Computing and Information Technology
Shaqra Universtiy

# TABLE OF CONTENT

# Chapter 1: Introduction

## 1.1 Definition of Cyber Threats

Cyber threats refer to any malicious activity or dangerous online content that can harm individuals or organizations. This includes a wide range of potential dangers, from cyberattacks that steal sensitive information to cyberbullying that can have devastating effects on young students and children.

### 1.1.1 Explanation of what constitutes a cyber threat

A cyber threat can take many forms, including viruses, malware, phishing scams, cyberbullying, identity theft, and more. It can originate from an individual, a group, or even a nation-state. The goal of a cyber threat is to gain unauthorized access to sensitive information, disrupt computer systems, or harm individuals.

## 1.1.2 Discussion of the different types of cyber threats

The types of cyber threats are constantly evolving, but some of the most common include:

- Phishing scams: Attempts to trick individuals into revealing sensitive information, such as passwords and credit card numbers, through emails or fake websites.

- Malware attacks: Attempts to install malicious software on a computer to gain access to sensitive information or disrupt computer systems.

- Cyberbullying: The use of technology, such as social media and texting, to harass, humiliate, or threaten individuals.

- Identity theft: The unauthorized use of someone's personal information, such as their name, Social Security number, or bank account information, to commit fraud.

## 1.2 Overview

Overview of the Book's Objectives and Purpose The primary goal of this book is to raise awareness about the dangers of cybercrime and to empower teachers, parents, and students with the skills and knowledge they need to stay safe online. The book is designed to provide a comprehensive guide to online safety, covering all the key aspects of cyber safety, from the latest technology and trends to practical tips and advice for preventing cyberattacks and protecting sensitive information.

### 1.2.1 Explanation of the book's primary goals

The primary goals of this book are to:

- Raise awareness about the dangers of cybercrime

- Empower teachers, parents, and students with the skills and knowledge they need to stay safe online

- Provide a comprehensive guide to online safety, covering all the key aspects of cyber safety

- Offer practical tips and advice for preventing cyberattacks and protecting sensitive information

### 1.2.2 Discussion of the book's target audience

The target audience of this book includes:

- Teachers

- Parents

- Students

- Anyone who is concerned about staying safe and secure online

### 1.2.3 Outline of the book's structure and contents

The book is structured into several chapters, each focusing on a different aspect of online safety. Chapter 2 covers the different types of cyber threats, including the latest technology and trends. Chapter 3 focuses on protecting yourself and your children online, including safe online practices, parental controls, and critical thinking and digital literacy skills. Chapter 4 empowers teachers and parents with the role they play in protecting young students and children from cyber threats. Chapter 5 emphasizes the importance of cybersecurity education and provides an overview of how to integrate it into the curriculum. Finally, Chapter 6 lists resources and support for anyone looking to stay safe and secure online.

# 2 Chapter 2: Types of Cyber Threats

## 2.1 Overview of Common Types of Cyberattacks

In the digital world, there are various types of cyberattacks that pose a threat to children and young students. In this section, we will discuss the three most common types of cyberattacks: phishing scams, malware attacks, and cyberbullying.

### 2.1.1 Discussion of Phishing Scams

Phishing scams are a type of cyber attack that seeks to trick individuals into revealing their personal and financial information. These scams can come in the form of emails, text messages, or phone calls that appear to be from a trustworthy source, such as a bank or government agency.

However, the information provided in the phishing email or message is usually false and used to steal sensitive information such as login credentials, Social Security numbers, or credit card information.

### 2.1.2 Explanation of Malware Attacks

Malware attacks are another common type of cyber attack that are designed to harm or disable computer systems and networks. This can include viruses, worms, Trojans, and other forms of malicious software that can infect a computer or device. Malware can be spread through email attachments, malicious websites, and other forms of digital communication. The consequences of malware attacks can include loss of sensitive information, identity theft, and other financial losses.

### 2.1.3 Overview of Cyberbullying

Cyberbullying is a type of online harassment that can occur on social media, instant messaging platforms, and other forms of digital communication. This type of bullying can be even more damaging than traditional bullying because it can reach a wider audience and be more difficult to escape from. Cyberbullying can take many forms, including insults, threats, and spreading rumors or false information about someone.

## 2.2 Discussion of the Latest Technology and Trends

The digital world is constantly evolving, with new technologies and trends emerging all the time. In this section, we will discuss the latest technology and trends, including social media, the Internet of Things, and other emerging technologies.

### 2.2.1 Overview of Social Media

Social media platforms, such as Facebook, Twitter, and Instagram, are becoming increasingly popular, especially among young people. While social media can be a fun and easy way to stay connected with friends and family, it can also pose a threat to young students and children. For example, they may be exposed to cyberbullying, be tricked into revealing personal information, or be vulnerable to other forms of cyber attacks.

### 2.2.2 Explanation of the Internet of Things

The Internet of Things (IoT) is the interconnectivity of physical devices and machines, allowing them to communicate and exchange data. This technology is becoming increasingly widespread and has the potential to change the way we live and work. However, it also creates new security challenges as many IoT devices may be vulnerable to hacking or cyber attacks.

### 2.2.3 Discussion of Other Emerging Technologies

Other emerging technologies, such as artificial intelligence and virtual reality, also have the potential to impact our lives in profound ways. However, these technologies also raise new security concerns, such as the risk of cyber attacks and loss of personal information.

# 2.3 Explanation of the Potential Consequences of Cyberattacks

The consequences of a cyberattack can be severe and long-lasting, affecting not only the individual targeted but also their family, friends, and wider community. Understanding the potential consequences of a cyberattack is crucial for preventing and protecting against these types of threats.

## 2.3.1 Discussion of identity theft

Identity theft occurs when someone gains access to sensitive personal information such as a person's name, address, social security number, or credit card information, and uses it to steal money or commit other crimes. The consequences of identity theft can be devastating, leading to financial loss, a damaged credit score, and a lot of time and effort to restore one's identity.

## 2.3.2 Explanation of loss of sensitive information

Cyberattacks can result in the loss of sensitive information, such as confidential business data, personal financial information, or intellectual property. The loss of sensitive information can cause significant harm to individuals, organizations, and even entire industries, as well as leading to legal and regulatory consequences.

### 2.3.3 Overview of other potential consequences

Cyberattacks can have far-reaching consequences, beyond the immediate loss of sensitive information or financial loss. For example, a cyberattack can disrupt a company's operations, causing financial damage and harm to its reputation, or it can compromise critical infrastructure, putting the safety and security of individuals at risk. Cyberattacks can also result in the spread of false information, causing harm to individuals, organizations, and even entire communities.

In conclusion, it is essential to understand the potential consequences of cyberattacks in order to take the necessary precautions to protect against them. From identity theft and the loss of sensitive information to the disruption of operations and the spread of false information, the consequences of cyberattacks can be far-reaching and long-lasting. By staying informed and taking proactive steps to protect against cyber threats, individuals, organizations, and communities can minimize the risks and consequences of cyberattacks.

# 3 Chapter 3: Protecting Yourself and Your Children Online

In Chapter 3 of the book, "Protecting Young Students and Children from Cyber Threats: A Comprehensive Guide to Online Safety," the focus shifts to the various steps individuals can take to stay safe online. This chapter provides practical tips and advice to help protect against cyber threats and keep sensitive information secure.

# 3.1 Discussion of Safe Online Practices

The first section of Chapter 3 is dedicated to discussing safe online practices that individuals can follow to stay safe from cyber threats. It provides an overview of the different measures that can be taken to protect against cybercrime.

### 3.1.1 Explanation of using strong passwords

One of the most important measures individuals can take to stay safe online is to use strong passwords. A strong password is one that is long and includes a mix of letters, numbers, and symbols. This makes it difficult for hackers to guess the password and gain access to sensitive information. Individuals are also advised to change their passwords regularly and not to use the same password for multiple accounts.

### 3.1.2 Discussion of avoiding suspicious emails

Another key aspect of staying safe online is avoiding suspicious emails. Individuals are advised to be cautious of emails that appear to come from unfamiliar sources, contain attachments, or ask for personal information. Phishing scams often use emails to trick individuals into providing their personal information, so it is important to be vigilant and avoid opening attachments or responding to emails from unknown sources.

### 3.1.3 Overview of other safe online practices

In addition to using strong passwords and avoiding suspicious emails, there are other online practices that individuals can follow to stay safe. For example, individuals are advised to be cautious when downloading software and apps and to avoid clicking on links from untrusted sources. They should also be careful when using public Wi-Fi and not to access sensitive information on public networks.

## 3.2 Explanation of Parental Controls

### 3.2.1 Discussion of the purpose of parental controls

Parental controls are tools and features that allow parents to monitor and restrict their children's access to certain content, websites, and apps. They can help parents protect their children from potential online dangers, such as cyberbullying, exposure to inappropriate content, or online predators.

### 3.2.2 Overview of different types of parental controls

There are several types of parental controls, including filtering software, time limits, and activity monitoring. Filtering software blocks certain types of content, such as explicit websites, while time limits allow parents to set limits on how much time their children can spend online. Activity monitoring allows parents to see what their children are doing online and to monitor their social media activity.

### 3.2.3 Explanation of how to set up and use parental controls

Parental controls can be set up through the device's operating system, such as Windows or Apple's iOS, or through third-party software. To set up parental controls, you'll need to create a separate user account for your child and then configure the settings to match your preferences. It's important to regularly check and adjust the parental controls as your child grows and their online behavior changes.

## 3.3 Discussion of Critical Thinking and Digital Literacy Skills

Critical thinking and digital literacy skills are essential in today's digital world in order to stay safe online. These skills allow individuals to evaluate online information, recognize potential dangers, and make informed decisions about their online behavior. In this section, the book discusses the importance of developing critical thinking and digital literacy skills in young students and children to help them navigate the digital world safely and responsibly.

### 3.3.1 Explanation of Evaluating Online Information

Evaluating online information is an important critical thinking skill that helps individuals determine whether a website, email, or social media post is trustworthy and reliable. This skill can help individuals identify potential scams, phishing attacks, and misinformation. The book provides tips for evaluating online information, such as checking the source of the information, looking for other sources to verify the information, and recognizing signs of bias or propaganda.

### 3.3.2 Overview of Recognizing Potential Dangers

Recognizing potential dangers online is another important critical thinking skill. This skill helps individuals identify malicious websites, suspicious emails, and other forms of cyberattacks. The book provides practical advice for recognizing potential dangers, such as being cautious of unexpected emails or social media messages, looking out for spelling and grammar errors in emails, and avoiding websites or downloads from untrusted sources.

### 3.3.3 Discussion of Other Critical Thinking and Digital Literacy Skills

In addition to evaluating online information and recognizing potential dangers, the book also discusses other critical thinking and digital literacy skills that are important for staying safe online. These skills include understanding the privacy settings on social media, avoiding oversharing personal information, and being cautious of the information that is shared or received online. The book provides practical tips and advice for developing these skills and using them to stay safe online.

In conclusion, critical thinking and digital literacy skills are essential for young students and children to stay safe and secure online. Through comprehensive coverage and practical tips, this section of the book empowers individuals with the skills and knowledge they need to navigate the digital world safely and responsibly.

# 4 Chapter 4: Empowering Teachers and Parents

## 4.1 Overview of the role of teachers and parents in protecting young students and children from cyber threats

In the digital world, teachers and parents play a critical role in protecting young students and children from cyber threats. They are responsible for promoting safe online habits and educating students and children about the dangers of cybercrime. Teachers and parents must work together to ensure the safety and security of students and children online.

### 4.1.1 Explanation of the importance of open communication and collaboration between teachers, parents, and children

Open communication and collaboration between teachers, parents, and children are essential for promoting cyber safety. Teachers and parents must establish a relationship of trust with students and children, encouraging them to share their online experiences and ask questions about cyber safety. By working together, teachers, parents, and children can create a safe and secure online environment.

### 4.1.2 Discussion of strategies for educating students and children about online safety and promoting safe online habits

Teachers and parents can educate students and children about online safety in a variety of ways. They can provide presentations, hold workshops, and incorporate cyber safety education into the curriculum. Additionally, they can encourage students and children to adopt safe online habits, such as using strong passwords, avoiding suspicious emails, and being mindful of their online activity.

## 4.2 The Role of Teachers in Cyber Safety

Teachers play a critical role in promoting cyber safety in schools. They are responsible for educating students about the dangers of cybercrime and empowering them with the skills and knowledge they need to stay safe online.

### 4.2.1 Explanation of the importance of cybersecurity education in schools

Cybersecurity education is essential in schools to ensure that students are equipped with the skills and knowledge they need to stay safe online. By teaching students about the dangers of cybercrime and promoting safe online habits, schools can reduce the risk of cyberattacks and protect sensitive information.

### 4.2.2 Discussion of how to integrate cybersecurity education into the classroom, including curriculum and lesson plans

Cybersecurity education can be integrated into the classroom through a variety of methods. It can be included in the regular curriculum, taught as a standalone course, or incorporated into existing courses such as computer science or technology. Teachers can use a variety of resources, such as lesson plans, activities, and assessments, to educate students about cyber safety.

### 4.2.3 Overview of teacher training and resources available for promoting cyber safety

There are a variety of resources available to support teachers in promoting cyber safety in the classroom. These resources include online courses, workshops, and professional development opportunities. Teachers can also access a variety of online resources, such as lesson plans and educational materials, to help them educate students about cyber safety.

# 4.3 The Role of Parents in Cyber Safety

Parents also play a critical role in protecting young students and children from cyber threats. They are responsible for monitoring their children's online activity and promoting safe online habits.

## 4.3.1 Explanation of the importance of monitoring children's online activity and setting up parental controls

Parents must monitor their children's online activity to ensure that they are engaging in safe and responsible behavior. This can be done by setting up parental controls and monitoring their children's social media accounts, email accounts, and other online activities.

## 4.3.2 Overview of parent resources available for promoting cyber safety

There are a variety of resources available to support parents in promoting cyber safety. These resources include online courses, workshops, and educational materials. Parents can also access a variety of online resources, such as tips and advice on promoting safe online habits, to help them educate their children about cyber safety.

# 5 Chapter 5:The Importance of Cybersecurity Education

In today's rapidly evolving digital world, it is more important than ever to ensure that young students and children are equipped with the skills and knowledge they need to stay safe online. One of the most effective ways of achieving this goal is through cybersecurity education, which provides individuals with the tools and information they need to stay safe from cyber threats.

## 5.1 Overview of the benefits of cybersecurity education

Cybersecurity education offers numerous benefits for individuals and society as a whole.

By providing young students and children with the skills and knowledge they need to stay safe online, the risk of cyberattacks can be significantly reduced. Additionally, digital literacy skills help individuals to navigate the digital world in a responsible and safe manner, promoting safe online habits and reducing the risk of cybercrime.

### 5.1.1 Discussion of the importance of reducing the risk of cyberattacks

Cybersecurity education is critical in reducing the risk of cyberattacks. By providing young students and children with the knowledge they need to identify and prevent cybercrime, the likelihood of falling victim to cyberattacks is greatly reduced. Additionally, cybersecurity education helps individuals to stay informed about the latest technology and trends, allowing them to keep up to date with the latest threats and make informed decisions about their online safety.

### 5.1.2 Explanation of the role of digital literacy in promoting safe online habits

Digital literacy is a key component of cybersecurity education, as it promotes safe online habits and helps individuals to navigate the digital world in a responsible and secure manner. By understanding how to evaluate online information and recognize potential dangers, individuals can make informed decisions about their online activities and protect themselves from cybercrime.

### 5.1.3 Overview of the benefits of cybersecurity education for individuals and society as a whole

Cybersecurity education provides numerous benefits for individuals and society as a whole. By reducing the risk of cyberattacks, individuals are better equipped to protect their personal information and sensitive data, reducing the risk of identity theft and loss of sensitive information. Additionally, cybersecurity education promotes critical thinking and digital literacy skills, helping individuals to navigate the digital world in a responsible and safe manner and contributing to a safer and more secure online environment for all.

## 5.2 Integrating Cybersecurity Education into the Curriculum

Cybersecurity education should be integrated into the curriculum in schools and institutions to ensure that young students and children are receiving the education they need to stay safe online. In this section, we will discuss curriculum options, the role of schools and institutions, and best practices for integrating cybersecurity education into the curriculum.

### 5.2.1 Overview of curriculum options for cybersecurity education

There are various options for integrating cybersecurity education into the curriculum. This can include dedicated courses, such as computer science and information technology, as well as incorporating cybersecurity topics into existing courses, such as social studies or science. In addition, schools and institutions can also provide workshops and extracurricular activities focused on cybersecurity education.

### 5.2.2 Discussion of the role of schools and institutions in promoting cyber safety education

Schools and institutions play a critical role in promoting cyber safety education. By incorporating cybersecurity education into the curriculum, they can ensure that young students and children are receiving the education they need to stay safe online. Additionally, schools and institutions can provide resources and support for teachers, parents, and students, to help them stay informed and up-to-date on the latest technology and trends in cybersecurity.

### 5.2.3 Explanation of best practices for integrating cybersecurity education into the curriculum

There are several best practices for integrating cybersecurity education into the curriculum. These include:

1. Incorporating cybersecurity topics into existing courses, such as social studies or science.
2. Providing dedicated courses or workshops focused on cybersecurity education.
3. Encouraging hands-on learning opportunities, such as computer programming or hacking simulations.
4. Integrating real-world examples and case studies into the curriculum to help students understand the practical implications of cybersecurity.
5. Partnering with organizations and experts in the field to provide resources and support for teachers and students.

## 5.3 Teacher Training and Support

### 5.3.1 Explanation of the importance of teacher training and support for promoting cyber safety education

The success of promoting cyber safety education and reducing the risk of cyberattacks among young students and children depends largely on the teachers who are responsible for imparting the knowledge and skills to these students. Teachers need to be well equipped and trained to effectively educate students about online safety and promote safe online habits. Therefore, it is important for teachers to receive the necessary training and support to be able to carry out their role effectively.

### 5.3.2  Overview of teacher training resources available

There are several resources available for teachers to receive training on promoting cyber safety education. Some of these resources include online courses, workshops, and training sessions, as well as professional development programs and conferences. These resources aim to provide teachers with the knowledge and skills they need to effectively educate students about online safety, as well as stay up-to-date with the latest technology and trends in the field.

### 5.3.3 Discussion of the role of professional development in promoting cyber safety education

Professional development plays a crucial role in promoting cyber safety education among teachers. By attending workshops, training sessions, and conferences, teachers are able to gain a deeper understanding of the latest technology and trends in the field, as well as best practices for promoting cyber safety education. Professional development also provides teachers with the opportunity to network with other professionals in the field and to collaborate on new and innovative ways to promote cyber safety education.

In conclusion, teacher training and support is a crucial component of promoting cyber safety education among young students and children. By providing teachers with the necessary training and resources, they are able to effectively educate students about online safety and reduce the risk of cyberattacks. This, in turn, leads to a safer and more secure online environment for everyone, including students, teachers, and the wider community. With ongoing professional development opportunities, teachers can continue to grow and enhance their knowledge and skills, leading to a more comprehensive and effective approach to cyber safety education.

# 6 Chapter 6: Resources and Support

## 6.1 List of Organizations and Websites for Cyber Safety

Information and Support In this chapter, we will provide a comprehensive list of organizations and websites dedicated to providing information and support for online safety and cybersecurity. These resources can be invaluable for teachers, parents, and students seeking to learn more about protecting themselves from cyber threats and promoting safe online habits.

### 6.1.1 Saudi CERT

In today's digital age, children are at risk of various cyber threats such as online harassment, cyber bullying, exposure to inappropriate content, and exploitation by online predators. It is important for teachers and parents to take the necessary precautions and educate children about safe online behavior.

Saudi CERT (Computer Emergency Response Team) is a national authority established under the National Cybersecurity Authority (NCA) in Saudi Arabia to raise cybersecurity awareness and protect the kingdom from cyber threats. It operates under Royal Decree 11/2/1439 and offers a range of services to individuals, organizations, and the government to stay protected against cyber threats.

Teachers and parents can report cyber threats to Saudi CERT or subscribe to its warnings and alerts to stay informed about the latest threats and vulnerabilities. The CERT also provides informative materials to educate individuals about cybersecurity and how to stay protected.

Saudi CERT is dedicated to raising awareness among children about cyber threats and how to stay protected. It provides educational materials and resources, such as videos, posters, and brochures, to help children understand safe and responsible online behavior where they can learn about cybersecurity, privacy, and online safety.

Saudi CERT is essential in protecting children from cyber threats in Saudi Arabia. Teachers and parents can rely on the CERT to provide the knowledge and skills needed to keep their children safe online. Saudi CERT offers a helpdesk, a range of resources to help families stay safe online.

### 6.1.2 National Initiative for Cybersecurity Education (NICE)

NICE is a partnership between government, academia, and the private sector aimed at promoting cybersecurity education and workforce development. NICE provides a variety of resources for educators and students, including lesson plans and curriculum resources for integrating cybersecurity education into the classroom.

### 6.1.3 Common Sense Media

Common Sense Media is a non-profit organization dedicated to promoting safe and responsible use of technology for children and families. The organization offers a wealth of information and resources for educators and parents, including tips for promoting safe online habits and advice on how to protect children from cyber threats.

## 6.2 Additional Support for Teachers, Parents, and Students

In addition to the organizations and websites listed above, there are a variety of other resources and support available for those seeking to protect themselves from cyber threats and promote safe online habits. These resources include online courses and training programs, workshops and events, and local and national initiatives aimed at promoting online safety and cybersecurity.

### 6.2.1 Online Courses and Training Programs

There are many online courses and training programs available for individuals seeking to learn more about online safety and cybersecurity. These programs can provide a comprehensive overview of common types of cyber threats, as well as practical tips and advice for protecting against them.

### 6.2.2 Workshops and Events

In addition to online resources, there are many workshops and events available for individuals seeking to learn more about online safety and cybersecurity. These events can provide hands-on training and practical advice for protecting against cyber threats and promoting safe online habits.

### 6.2.3 Local and National Initiatives

There are many local and national initiatives aimed at promoting online safety and cybersecurity, including community outreach programs, local schools, and government agencies. These initiatives can provide valuable information and support for individuals seeking to learn more about protecting themselves from cyber threats and promoting safe online habits.

In conclusion, this chapter has outlined a variety of resources and support available for individuals seeking to protect themselves from cyber threats and promote safe online habits. From national organizations and online courses, to workshops and local initiatives, there is a wealth of information and support available for teachers, parents, and students looking to stay safe and secure online.